Independent Shops
London

INDEPENDENT SHOPS LONDON

Michelle Mason

About the Author

Michelle Mason is a designer, photographer and stylist and the vintage buyer for a number of clients including the Sir John Soane's Museum shop. She has created vintage pop-up shops for Kew Gardens and the Southbank Centre and is the owner of east London vintage showroom and online store, Mason & Painter.

Independent Shops London is Michelle's fourth book and follows on from *Vintage Shops London* and *Love Vintage*.

Contents

Introduction

Rumour had it that Napoleon called the English, 'a nation of shopkeepers'. In reality it seems the quote was never genuinely recorded, but fake or not it seems apt for a nation that produces very good shopkeepers.

As a London-based shopkeeper for over ten years, I love to visit other independent shops. I'm lured with childlike anticipation by the promise of finding something unusual or unexpected. I'm also secure in the knowledge that the same experience and service is rarely found in big brand, mass market stores.

Whether it's the local art supplier, the deli round the corner, or a favourite clothing boutique, the setting and the narrative is one-of-a-kind and uniquely personal to each and every shop.

I can spend hours dipping in and out of beautiful – and useful – small shops because I appreciate the time and hard work that goes into stocking, styling and presenting everything on offer. In *Independent Shops London* I feature 50 of my favourite shops and independent markets around the capital – paying homage to the individuals and small teams who pore their all into their businesses.

Arranged by area – north, east, south, west and central – each section has a selection of shop types and includes places of interest where applicable. I've enjoyed featuring established and popular favourites as well as a new wave of businesses opening their doors to customers, who like myself enjoy supporting independent retailers and prefer to shop small.

Why shop small?

Why, you might ask, would you pay slightly more in a small, independent shop when larger retailers or chains offer items for less? The answer to that is simple: the high street needs small shops to survive and thrive.

Without independent shops our town centres and high streets would look very different. A slump in the economy, rent and rate increases and online shopping all affect small retailers. The local cafés, grocers, hardware shops and independent bookshops would all but disappear if we turned our backs on them.

When we shop small we experience meaningful, real-life encounters with shopkeepers who know their stock inside out. They can trace locally sourced produce, often naming the grower or maker, or recount the history behind each product. Their expert knowledge and personal touches are priceless.

By supporting independent shops we give agency to the small producers, makers, chefs and designers who contribute to make each shop – and high street – unique.

EAST LONDON

LF Markey

50 Dalston Lane, E8 3AH
www.lfmarkey.com

Womenswear & Accessories

LF Markey, at number 50 Dalston Lane, is a joy to visit. The multi-coloured collection of dungarees, boiler suits and dresses in bright, bold fabrics light up the storefront regardless of the London rain.

Louise Markey, ex-Burberry designer, has a penchant for classic workwear and up-beat modern designs. The instantly recognisable prints, confident silhouettes and utility style classics follow a slow approach to fashion with sustainable materials and ethical manufacture.

The store is now set to launch a range of textiles and ceramics in their trademark juicy fruit colours and perky patterns – perfect additions for dedicated LF Markey fans.

Violet Cakes

47 Wilton Way, E8 3ED
www.violetcakes.com

Bakery

Originally from California, Claire Ptak, honed her skills in the kitchen of pioneering chef, Alice Waters. After a move to London in 2005, Claire rented a stall on Broadway Market, a favourite east London foodie hangout, selling her homemade cakes each Saturday alongside cheesemakers, costermongers and pop-up coffee shops.

When the demand for Claire's confections called for a bricks and mortar premises she opened Violet bakery and café, just a short stroll across London Fields from her original market stall. Organic and low intervention ingredients are Violet's USP. Elderflowers, apples, Kentish cherries, London quinces, Yorkshire rhubarb and Herefordshire berries are used to create a variety of delicious fillings and pastel coloured creams.

Their vegan California Cake – a nod to Claire's west coast roots – is just one of the popular made-to-order celebration cakes, filled and iced with their to-die-for buttercream and topped with organic flowers.

Situated on a quiet Victorian Street, minutes from the bustle of Dalston Junction, Violet's is the perfect spot for afternoon tea. Sit with a book, a pot of your favourite brew and a cupcake fresh from the glass shop counter.

Milagros

61 Columbia Road, E2 7RG
www.milagros.co.uk

Mexican Homeware

When Juliette went looking for handmade glassware, her search led to Milagros, a Bristol-based Mexican shop. As she boarded the train at Paddington station over twenty-five years ago, she never imagined that she'd find her dream products – and end up building a life with Tom, the shop owner.

Tom relocated to London and, together with Juliette, they opened the Columbia Road shop to specialize in Mexican crafts and handmade homewares. Tom sources each item and works closely with the small, independent makers, travelling to Mexico every twelve months or so. Juliette takes care of the retail and social media side of the business.

Their inviting yellow-painted shop front leads to a vast assortment of hand blown glassware, baskets, ceramics and Day of the Dead papier-mâché decorations. Handmade encaustic tiles are available in an assortment of folksy patterns and colours and Milagros offer helpful installation advice on all projects

Yeast

Unit 1 Canal Place, 1–3 Sheep Lane, E8 4QS
www.yeastbakery.com

Bakery

Initially supplying viennoiserie and bread to trade, Yeast Bakery only opened its shutters to the public at weekends, selling artisan pastries, breads and takeaway coffee from a railway arch in east London.

In 2021, owners Ben and Angela took the plunge and graduated to a smart canal-side café, bakery and lifestyle shop, down the road from their original premises. With Ben and the team busy in the open plan kitchen, and Angela running front-of-house, they now serve up their delicious pastries, savouries and coffee five days a week to the local folk of Hackney (bread available Saturdays), offering sit-in breakfast, brunch, lunch and coffee.

What makes Yeast bakery so special? Just one bite of their handmade, caramel cream brioche and you'll see why.

Studio Wylder

67 Columbia Road, E2 7RG
www.studiowylder.com

Womenswear

With a background in fashion and over thirty years working with international fashion houses, Natasha – founder of Studio Wylder – felt ready to move into her own bricks and mortar premises after a successful run of pop-up shops.

When a shop in the neighbourhood became available, Natasha took a leap of faith and applied for the lease. She picked up the keys in time to launch the Summer 2023 collection and her locally-made designs immediately caught the eye of fashion savvy women.

Organic linen, natural Kala cotton and overstock sheepskin are used to create tailored jackets, fluid maxi dresses and trousers in classic wearable colours of oatmeal, navy, black and taupe. If you're looking for mindfully made, modern pieces, a visit to Studio Wylder won't disappoint.

Broadway Market

London, E8
www.broadwaymarket.co.uk

Food & Craft Market

It's said that this long established street market inspired the creators of the TV soap, Eastenders. And although the market goes back many decades, its current incarnation as a destination for street food and organic produce is hugely popular with locals and visitors alike.

Every Saturday, from early morning until dusk, stalls line the street to offer a diverse selection of culinary delights – from Indian and Vietnamese street food to French crêpes and patisserie, organic vegetables, Italian olives, local cheeses and bread. You'll also find a good selection of crafts from makers selling homewares, jewellery, artwork, clothing and ceramics.

A favourite Saturday morning is a slow wander round the market with coffee and something sweet, followed by a browse in one of the three bookshops along the street. If you're feeling energetic, a stroll round nearby London Fields and back towards Broadway Market for a local pint in The Five Points Brewery, 61 Mare Street, is a great way to see this vibrant east London neighbourhood.

Columbia Road Flower Market

Columbia Road, E2 7RG
www.columbiaroadmarket.co.uk

Flower Market

This pretty slice of east London, lined with independent shops, bars and cafés, was destined for demolition in the 1970s. Local residents and shopkeepers petitioned to save the Victorian street but the original Columbia Market – a stately building with space to house 400 market traders – didn't survive the bulldozers. Flower vendors, undeterred and eager to carry on trading, set up a regulated street market in the 1960s, laying the foundations for this ever-popular Sunday market.

Today, Columbia Road Flower Market draws visitors from all corners of the world as well as photographers, film crews and locals enjoying the atmosphere and shopping for plant bargains. Every Sunday from 7am to 3pm, rain or shine, you'll find fresh flowers, herbs, bedding plants, bulbs, houseplants and trees such as olive, bay, lemon and orange.

Take the train to Liverpool Street station or tube to Bethnal Green and make a beeline for the horticultural splendour and independent shops lining the road. Arrive early if crowds aren't your thing (it gets busy by 10am), and pick up a coffee and a bagel from one of the cafés such as Cafe Columbia at number 138 or Jack Garcia at number 150.

Pocket of Interest
Columbia Road

Columbia Road, E2
www.columbiaroad.info

Columbia Road is one of the last streets in London to remain wholly independent and owes much of its renown to the shops that line the street. Sunday is their main trading day, though some shops are open Wednesday through to the weekend. From gifts, jewellery, vinyl and antiques to womenswear, childrenswear, homewares and pet supplies, there's something for everyone.

Bob & Blossom

140 Columbia Road, E2 7RG
www.bobandblossom.co.uk

Children's Clothing & Toys

With its timeless shop interior, vintage till and reclaimed counter, Bob & Blossom effortlessly mixes toy shop nostalgia and charm with good quality new products for children up to the age of five.

Pastel coloured crates filled with pocket money toys, shelves of furry animals, retro Dinky cars and lace tutus, sit alongside Bob & Blossom's own range of cutesy, striped sweatshirts for children and toddlers.

For over twenty years Bob & Blossom's owner, Kirsten, has stocked her Columbia Road shop with irresistible children's books, clothing, accessories, gift wrap and cards. If you're on the hunt for baby gifts Bob & Blossom has the coolest all-in-ones, hats and t-shirts.

Conservatory Archives

3–7 Lower Clapton Road, E5 0NS
www.conservatoryarchives.co.uk

Plants

Walk through the door of Conservatory Archives and you're immediately transported to a green oasis that cleverly combines potting shed appeal with Victorian greenhouse vibes. From floor to ceiling, a mesmerizing tangle of stems, leaves, fronds and giant cacti are arranged between vintage sofas and reclaimed sinks and tables to create a calming, horticultural welcome.

Owners Jin and Giacomo have built up an enviable collection of plants of all shapes, sizes and origins, from dangly succulents in pots to beautiful broad leafed tropicals and elegant palms – none of which would look out of place in the hothouse at Kew Gardens.

Knowledgeable staff are on hand to help with plant advice and there's a good selection of terracotta pots, planters, hanging baskets, soil and plant food to cultivate your own indoor jungle.

The Deli Downstairs

211 Victoria Park Road, E9 7JN
www.thedelidownstairs.co.uk

Grocery

The term sustainable couldn't be more relevant to The Deli Downstairs. Selling more than just groceries, The Deli is a village shop supplying seasonal food, locally-made bread, British and continental cheeses and organic eggs. Fresh fruit and vegetables are sourced from small growers and a local florist is on hand twice a week with seasonal, British-grown blooms.

The Deli also offers the option to re-fill recycled bottles and containers with eco cleaning products, wine and milk. Their locally-roasted, takeaway coffee is supplied in a 'rent-a-cup', since owner Sophie had had enough of sweeping discarded paper cups off the pavement.

Located in the pretty Victoria Park Village, there's plenty of seating under the stretch of red and white awnings to sit and watch the world go by with a morning latte and a freshly baked croissant.

The Mercantile

17a Lamb Street, E1 6EA
www.themercantilelondon.com

Womenswear & Accessories

If you're in the market for eclectic womenswear and ace accessories, one trip to The Mercantile is all it takes to have you hooked. Owners Debra and Rebecca buy their collections from small independent labels in Scandinavia, France, Belgium and the UK, and offer a conscious edit of some of the coolest contemporary designs available.

With regular trips to Paris, Oslo and Copenhagen, their handpicked selections mix mindful, contemporary clothes with a chic, fresh vibe from both emerging and established brands.

The Mercantile is the antithesis of high street chains and you get the feeling that the staff love working in such a fun, relaxed environment. But be warned, this shop doesn't do run of the mill. If you're okay with that then you're in for a treat.

Colours of Arley

61 Hackney Road, E2 7NX
www.coloursofarley.com

Interiors

It all started when proprietor Louisa went in search of stripy fabrics for her Patterdale terrier's bed. Unable to find what she was looking for, she tested her own designs at the family printing workshop in Cheshire. The results were so good that friends begged for the colourful stripes for their own homes and Colours of Arley launched in 2022.

The Hackney HQ occupies a light filled corner shop where customers are encouraged to choose colour combinations – with endless possibilities – from 180 swatches displayed on the wall. Each personalized fabric is then printed to order: from bright deckchair stripes to subtle pastels, traditional or kitsch – the choice is entirely yours.

And if you're in need of ideas, there's plenty of cushions, lampshades and upholstery examples to kickstart your look book. One thing's for sure, you'll feel like the proverbial kid in the candy shop at Colours of Arley.

Right: Colour swatches line the wall for bespoke striped or checked fabrics produced at the family workshops in Cheshire.

WEST LONDON

Papersmiths

170 Pavilion Road, SW1X 0AW
www.papersmiths.co.uk

Stationery

Sidonie Warren, Papersmiths founder, started her business after an unconventional career path eventually led to graphic design. Working from a studio in Bristol, passersby would ask if they could buy the items displayed in the windows. 'We just had these nice things around the studio,' says Sidonie, 'but we needed to pay the rent and so we decided to turn half the space into a bricks and mortar shop.'

It was the catalyst for a new venture and it made sense to focus on stationery, a passion since childhood. The Bristol store subsequently moved to Brighton. In 2021 Papersmiths opened a second shop in London.

Decorated in vivid citrusy colours, the Chelsea boutique is choc-full of products sourced from designers and makers around the world. Fill up on classic cult pens, classy greetings cards, journals, gift wrap, pencil cases and diaries. And now, with their own-brand products, Papersmiths is a stationery addicts dream in full technicolour. My advice? Only visit after pay day.

Summerill & Bishop

100 Portland Road, W11 4LQ
and 58 Elizabeth Street, SW1W 9PB
www.summerillandbishop.com

Kitchenware & Homeware

Best friends, home cooks and entertainers, June Summerill and Bernadette Bishop were frustrated by the lack of decent, beautiful kitchenware and so founded their Clarendon Cross shop in 1994.

Over thirty years later, Summerill & Bishop has evolved and grown to include a second shop in Belgravia and a devoted following. They are best known for their sought-after tablecloths and bespoke linens. Choose from art deco-inspired Italian linen, stripy linen tea towels and napkins personalized with initials.

Both shops are immaculately styled with quality crafted tableware. Every item, from eggcups to glass candelabras, is both functional and beautiful. If you only come away with one thing, make it the recyclable plastic water jug in teal blue.

David Mellor

190 Pavilion Road, SW3 2BF
www.davidmellordesign.com

Tableware & Kitchenware

David Mellor isn't new to Chelsea, on the contrary, their classic mid-century designed cutlery and kitchenware is as popular today as it was when the shop first opened in 1969, a stone's throw from Sloane Square.

The handsome green-painted shop was originally built as a fire station and recently restored by Corin Mellor and his team of designers. Bespoke fixtures and fittings were made in their Derbyshire cutlery factory to create a seamless fit for the sophisticated range of home and kitchen essentials.

David Mellor (1930–2009) was awarded Royal Designer for Industry so it's no surprise to learn that his collections of homewares and industrial designs are exhibited in museums and honoured with countless awards. Mellor's iconic designs include the national traffic light system, the red square post box and the Abacus bus shelter.

The Pavilion Road shop stocks a wide selection of tableware, glassware and ceramics as well as kitchen knives and cookware. My favourite? The silver plate, Pride cutlery set, designed in 1953 and still in production today.

Papers & Paints

4 Park Walk, SW10 0AD
www.papersandpaints.co.uk

Paint & Colour Specialists

Just off Fulham Road, sandwiched between an art gallery and a wedding dress shop, this long established paint and colour specialist has been mixing paint from the same address since 1960. Now run by husband-and-wife team, Alex and Patrick Baty, Papers & Paints was originally founded by Patrick's father, Robert.

Known to interior decorators as the industry go-to for specialist and heritage colours, Papers & Paints mix their 'colour recipes' in-house and have paint matched for English Heritage, numerous stately homes and Tower Bridge, to name a few.

Their colour card sample sets, which include Neoclassical, Colours of the 1920s, French Exteriors, Great Halls and the Best of the 1960s, means there's something to inspire any mood board or renovation project.

Ceramica Blue

10 Blenheim Crescent, W11 1NN
www.ceramicablue.co.uk

Tableware & Kitchenware

Entering Ceramica Blue is like stepping off a plane into warm sunshine – even in the depths of a British winter. This lifestyle and tableware shop sells the type of stylish glassware and serveware that you'd fall in love with on a Mediterranean holiday.

Lindy Wiffen opened Ceramica Blue in 1987 with brightly coloured, hand decorated plates and jugs from Sicily. Those same eclectic ceramics are still as popular today, although Ceramica Blue's range has grown to include hand blown glass from Murano, Portuguese dinnerware, Indonesian cookware, Swedish linen and vases made in Devon.

Located in the heart of Notting Hill and adjacent to Portobello market, Ceramica Blue is a must for anyone looking for unusual wedding gifts and quality kitchenware.

Lutyens & Rubinstein

21 Kensington Park Road, W11 2EU
www.landrbookshop.co.uk

Books

The core collection of this Notting Hill bookshop was built on reader recommendations. Contacts, publishers and friends of all ages were asked for their suggestions or to nominate their favourite reads.

Founded by literary agents, Sarah Lutyens and Felicity Rubinstein, this welcoming and well-stocked bookshop has a dedicated children's area and a poetry and art section, as well as popular non-fiction and fiction titles. There's also a good selection of stationery and reading glasses.

If you're looking for a wedding list book service, gift ideas for important birthdays or a housewarming, L & R offer tailor-made personalized lists – complete with bookplates and gift notes.

Canford & Co

307 Lillie Road, SW6 7LL
www.canfordframes.co.uk

Picture Framers

Annabelle and Lucy met at school and remained in touch throughout their various travels. With backgrounds in art and design, it was their shared love of fine art and vintage that sealed the idea of setting up a picture framing workshop in Fulham's Lillie Road, surrounded by antiques shops and art galleries.

Their bespoke frames mean that every job is tailored to individual artwork and when it comes to attention to detail, Canford & Co is in a league of its own. Triple mounts, gilded, stained or hand painted – no request, it seems, is beyond their ability.

The workshop also doubles as a beautifully curated shop where French dressers display pre-loved tableware, decorative antiques and a good selection of ready-framed prints and paintings.

Tables and dressers display collections of vintage ceramics alongside framed prints and paintings. With Mabel, page 56, and Betty, right.

John Sandoe Books

10–12 Blacklands Terrace, SW3 2SR
www.johnsandoe.com

Books

John Sandoe Books has been in the same Chelsea street, at the top of King's Road, since 1957. Feeling more like a private library than a bookshop, the atmosphere is cosy old-fashioned charm with its creaky floorboards, vases of fresh flowers, Persian rugs and bookshelves that look as though they've existed for centuries. But don't be fooled by the quaint Miss Marple appeal. John Sandoe's is a seriously good bookshop stocked with over 30,000 books from the latest in fiction, lifestyle and the arts to children's books, cookery, gardening and music.

This three-storey independent shop is a booklover's dream. The staff are super friendly and with books to tempt you on table tops, counters, chairs and even on the staircase, you'll never want to leave.

M Charpentier

284 Lillie Road, SW6 7PX
www.mcharpentier.com

Antiques

Sisters Camilla and Alix Charpentier have a reputation for sourcing quality antiques and furniture ranging from the eighteenth to twentieth century. Mostly sourced from the brocantes of France, their collections are both eclectic and diverse.

With a knack for mixing a variety of pieces, Charpentier's stock includes antique garden ornaments, vintage lighting, mid-century furniture and antique mirrors and paintings – all lovingly restored and ready to enjoy at home.

Whether you're the owner of a chateau or a mid-century apartment there's something to suit every interior style.

CENTRAL LONDON

Paul Rothe & Son

35 Marylebone Lane, W1U 2NN
@paulrotheandson

Delicatessen

Rothe's has been a central London mainstay for the best part of 125 years and serving up deli lunches and hot drinks to go for the past sixty years.

Originally founded as a grocery store, this quaint, double-fronted shop has been in the same family for four generations. Today, Paul Rothe's great grandson Stephen greets customers with a cheery smile and an extensive choice of fresh, made-to-order sandwiches, salads and homemade soups.

Snuggle into one of the retro-style Formica booths, surrounded by jars of British staples such as piccalilli, Marmite and mustard, and fill up on lunchtime favourites like egg mayo or cheese and pickle. Or join the early bird breakfast crew from 8.30am and soak up the cosy, welcoming ambience as the rest of London wakes up.

Postcard Teas

9 Dering Street, W1S 1AG
www.postcardteas.com

Teas

Step into Postcard Teas and despite its central location, you're instantly struck by a zen-like calm. The neat boutique-style emporium, just off Bond Street, offers over seventy speciality teas, attractively packaged and displayed in postcard-size boxes with vintage-style graphics.

The company's three proprietors, hailing from China, Japan and Britain, have over thirty years of expertise between them, as well as clocking up multiple trips to tea-growing regions, hence their name.

Postcard sources its tea from micro farms – on average the size of just two football pitches – to support local growers and guarantee small-scale production. Closer to home, each batch is roasted, packed and labelled with the maker's details in their Camden warehouse. So, if you like to know where your cuppa was grown and by whom, then head over to this unique specialist store for a truly ethical brew.

O Pioneers

76 Marylebone Lane, W1U 2PR
www.opioneers.co.uk

Womenswear

Best friends Clara and Tania came up with the idea for a grown-up fashion label while walking their dogs on Hampstead Heath. Clara, an actor, and Tania, with a background in PR, wanted to move away from fast fashion and focus on creating British-made timeless pieces to be enjoyed every day rather than saved for best.

End-of-line fabrics and past season Liberty prints are used to create O Pioneers signature vintage-inspired collections. Choose from one of their heritage print dresses or retro-inspired tank tops, knitted by a small team of women including Clara and Tania's mums.

The eminently pretty clothes – think *Little House on the Prairie* – perfectly reflect Clara and Tania's *joie de vivre*. With plenty of limited editions and one-off items, there's more than enough to tempt you, whatever the season.

David Penton & Son

64 Marylebone Lane, W1U 2PE
www.pentonshardware.co.uk

Hardware

There's an old-worldy feel about Penton's hardware shop yet it's only a stone's throw from the traffic jams and chain stores on Oxford Street. Brimming with a miscellany of household gadgets and tools, from fixtures for a plumbing emergency to electrical goods, cleaning supplies and a wide range of brushes and brooms, you'll chance upon all sorts of useful items.

Surrounded by restaurants with pavement tables, a ribbon shop and a traditional pub, the area has a much slower pace than your average west end postcode. Cliff and his colleagues are at the ready to help with any requests and know their stock inside out. Visit Penton's if you're in the neighbourhood, treat yourself to a beechwood nailbrush or a pair of quality Japanese secateurs and lap up the Marylebone Village vibe.

Sir John Soane's Museum Shop

13 Lincoln's Inn Fields, WC2A 3BP
www.soane.org

Gifts

Housed in a spectacular trio of Georgian buildings Sir John's Soane's Museum was once home to celebrated British architect Sir John Soane, designer of the Bank of England and Dulwich Picture Gallery, amongst other architectural gems.

Soane created a museum for his collection of antiquities and paintings so it's no surprise that the museum's shop is stocked with items of architectural and design interest. With its marble fireplace, crystal chandelier and selection of useful and unusual gifts the shop is a joy to visit.

There's something to suit all pockets, from books on architecture and Georgian history to classical plaster cast busts, maps of Regency London, Hogarth prints and jewellery inspired by the museum's collections.

This centrally located museum behind Holborn tube station, houses a multitude of historical treasures including 30,000 architectural drawings, Hogarth's series *A Rake's Progress* and ancient Egyptian artefacts – all of which are free to visit. You can, of course, support the museum shop before you leave and snap up a quirky head of Apollo vase or a pair of Bank of England earrings.

L Cornelissen & Son

105 Great Russell Street
WC1B 3RW

www.cornelissen.com

Art supplies

Louis Cornelissen opened his original Covent Garden shop in the 1850s and established himself as an Artist's Colourman and supplier of brushes, canvases, printing materials and fine papers.

For over 120 years the shop remained a family business until Nicolas Walt relocated the shop to its current Bloomsbury address, a short stroll from the British Museum.

Cornelissen's extensive range of gilding and restoration materials, pencils, pastels, inks, tubes of paint and glass jars filled with pigments are proudly on display in smart, museum-worthy black fittings, with numbered drawers floor to ceiling. Even if you're not on the hunt for artist's materials, this long-established shop sells beautiful marbled papers, books and gift sets for the arty friends in your life.

Panter & Hall

22–24 Cecil Court, WC2N 4HE
(also at 21–22 Pall Mall, SW1Y 5LP)
www.panterandhall.com

Art dealers

Behind the elegant Edwardian shopfronts at numbers 22–24 Cecil Court, you'll find art dealers Panter & Hall Decorative. In business for over thirty years, Tiffany Panter and Matthew Hall specialize in contemporary 'affordable art' and mid-twentieth-century paintings.

The shop interior, with its stacks of canvases, dark wooden panelling and black marble fireplaces, wouldn't look out of place in a period drama yet the exhibitions and ever-changing collections feel upbeat and fresh.

For bargains, rummage through the stock of old picture frames and catalogues on the pavement outside or check out the impressive collection of mid-century art. The regular exhibitions from their stable of contemporary artists are also well worth a visit.

Pocket of Interest
Cecil Court

WC2

www.cecilcourt.co.uk

Once known as Flicker Alley, in reference to its links with early British film pioneers, and attracting past famous residents including Mozart, T S Elliot and Ellen Terry, Cecil Court has had its fair share of historical claims to fame.

At the epicentre of Theatreland, stretching between Charing Cross Road and St Martins Lane, this pedestrian-only alley has charm in spadefuls. It's easy to see why the street is an Instagram favourite – it's also said that Diagon Alley, the Harry Potter hangout, was partly inspired by Cecil Court.

Nowadays art dealers and antiquarian bookshops rub shoulders with other special interest shops selling antique maps, banknotes, coins, vintage children's books and the long established ballet shop, Freed, on the corner at 94 St Martins Lane.

Mr Jones Watches

53a Neal Street, WC2H 9PJ
www.mrjoneswatches.com

Watches

This boutique-style shop, with its illustrated walls and breezy decor perfectly matches the brand's mood for cool quality and hip design. The off-beat interior, with a wall of magnifying glasses to view the watches, wouldn't look out of place on the set of a Wes Anderson movie.

Crispin Jones, founding director and one of several designers at Mr Jones, opened the Covent Garden store in 2024 to showcase the bespoke collection of watches. Crispin says, 'We don't follow trends. We make unusual watches which tell a story and start a conversation.'

Crafted and assembled in the UK, each watch is designed with a unique hand-printed face; the result of collaborations with artists to create the exclusive, playful designs.

Put Mr Jones at the top of your shopping list if you're in the market for a new watch or special gift. Also check out their co-ordinated range of artist-illustrated tee shirts while you're there.

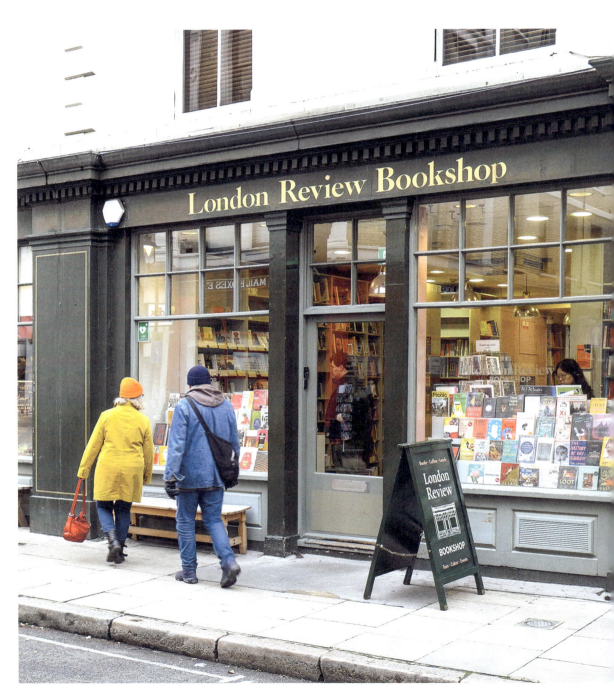

London Review Bookshop

14 Bury Place, WC1A 2JL
www.londonreviewbookshop.co.uk

Books

The *London Review of Books* literary magazine may well be on your radar but did you know they also have a central London bookshop? The welcoming, spacious shop stocks over 20,000 books and pleasant staff are happy to help with enquiries or reading requests.

Tucked down a tranquil Bloomsbury street, minutes from the queues circling the British Museum, this central hub offers a wide variety of titles from international classics to contemporary fiction, science, cookery, poetry, philosophy and children's books. With plenty of benches and access to an outdoor yard, the bookshop is the perfect place to spend a lunch hour and stock up on favourite authors.

La Fromagerie

52 Lamb's Conduit Street, WC1N 3LL
www.lafromagerie.co.uk

Cheesemonger

La Fromagerie's founder, Patricia Michelson, started selling cheese from her garden shed after falling in love with the local fromage whilst on holiday in the French Alps. Twelve months later, she moved to a stall in Camden market, followed by her first shop in Highbury.

Today there are three London locations representing cheesemaking talent from around Europe, as well as British and Irish cheese and La Fromagerie's own label wines and condiments.

Fill your boots with delights from the pantry-style cheeseroom or spend time in the restaurant, which serves breakfast through to supper as well as cheese-tasting events and courses (bookable online for the Highbury and Marylebone locations).

In addition to the cheeseroom, you'll find local bread and seasonal fruit and vegetables. Staff are on hand to help pair your cheese purchases with wine or any number of accompaniments such as truffle honey, damson paste or oat biscuits.

A favourite with London restauranteurs and cheese lovers, La Fromagerie stock their largest selection of cheese at the Marylebone flagship store, 2–6 Moxon Street, W1U 4EW. Their original, north London shop is at 30 Highbury Park, London N5 2AA.

Wild at Heart

Liberty, Great Marlborough Street, W1B 5AH
www.wildatheart.com

Florist

For over twenty-five years, flower powerhouse Nikki Tibbles and her team of expert florists have created opulent, sought-after floral designs for weddings and special events. The original Wild at Heart flagship shop in Notting Hill has become an institution with a reputation for beautiful bouquets.

In 2008 Wild At Heart was selected by Liberty to flank the entrance to the iconic department store and it's easy to understand how this stretch of pavement has become an Instagram favourite. Fresh hand-tied bouquets, plants and tubs of seasonal flowers greet visitors to the world-renowned west end store on a daily basis.

Wild at Heart continues to inspire with its artful designs and is a perfect match for Liberty's design heritage.

NORTH LONDON

My Little Garden

158 Liverpool Rd, Old Concertina Works, N1 1LA
@mylittlegardenlondon

Florist

'It must be the smallest shop in London,' declares Deb, owner of My Little Garden. Not much bigger than a garden shed, what this flower shop lacks in space it makes up for in the stylish arrangements of fresh British flowers.

An old concertina works forms part of Deb's home and served as a shop window for her artist husband's paintings. When Deb started to supply flowers to a community food shop during lockdown, friends suggested she should sell her floral arrangements alongside the paintings.

My Little Garden now caters for all events including birthdays and weddings, as well as bouquets for regular customers and passersby attracted by the seasonal flowers in the open windows. Expect wild, country flowers and natural foliage freshly sourced from local growers.

Loop

15 Camden Passage, N1 8EA
www.loopknitting.com

Knitting & Haberdashery

Voted best Independent Knitting Shop in London, it's easy to see why Loop London has gained a cult following amongst knitters, embroiderers and makers. An extensive range of yarns, patterns and knitting ephemera is lovingly displayed over two floors of an Edwardian premises in Camden Passage – a quaint pedestrian-only alley, fringed with cosy cafés and vintage shops.

Loop's founder, Susan Cooper, set up shop over fifteen years ago with a desire to offer expert advice and knitting workshops alongside hand-dyed yarns and natural fibres from around the world. On the ground floor you'll find haberdashery and shelves loaded with a kaleidoscope of coloured yarns, as well as exclusive heirloom designs from independent makers. Venture upstairs for vintage haberdashery, knitted baby clothes, ribbons, buttons and craft books with a snug sofa for reading up on techniques and ideas.

Susan's staff are expert knitters and on the day I visited, at least three members of the team were wearing their own creations. Proof, if needed, that Loop London are passionate about their work.

N1 Garden Centre

25A Englefield Road, N1 4EU
www.n1gardencentre.co.uk

Garden Centre

Within walking distance to the city of London, this award-winning garden centre is a calm, green space teeming with ferns, annual flowers, shrubs, citrus trees and houseplants. And no matter if London living means your outdoor space is limited to a balcony or windowsill, there's plenty of inspiration with displays for patios and container gardens.

There's also an impressive selection of indoor plants and tropicals in the original Victorian, light-filled building. Giant monsteras, banana plants, succulents, palms and *ficus*, to name just a few, are arranged with a wide selection of planters, pots, tubs and hanging baskets.

With weekly deliveries of fresh, seasonal stock there's ample choice for gardens of all sizes, from perennials, climbers, bedding plants and herbs to a wide selection of seeds, compost and feeds.

Whether you're creating a garden from scratch or planting up a window box a visit to N1 is essential, if only for the inspiration and helpful suggestions from friendly staff.

Jessica de Lotz

49 Fortess Rd, London NW5 1AD
www.jessicadelotz.co.uk

Jewellery

Drawing on inspiration from vintage books, wax seals, love letters and found objects at antiques fairs, Jessica de Lotz has carved a rightful niche in the market for highly original, handmade jewellery. Memories, nostalgia and storytelling are finely woven into each collection and clients often revisit to invest in pendants or rings stamped with their initials, special dates or bespoke designs.

Whether it's a love locket necklace, a zodiac charm or a personalized bracelet, Jessica creates each unique piece with the customer in either gold, rose gold or silver. There's also a wide selection of ready-to-wear jewellery including the popular arrow earrings, handcuff necklace, moodstone rings and mini hand bangles.

And you'd be right in thinking you've spotted Jessica's originals on the big screen. Her wax seal rings have made an appearance in the TV drama, *House of the Dragon* and in the 2019 film *Little Women*; all of which are available in the Kentish Town shop or made-to-order with custom engraving.

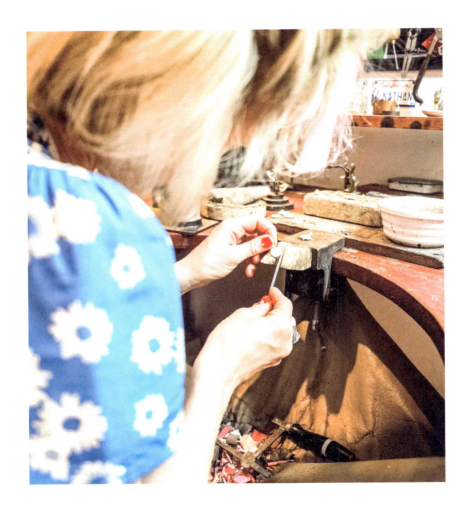

Know & Love

176 Stoke Newington Church Street, N16 0JL
www.knowandlove.co.uk

Homeware

Every product chosen by Karen Sims for her beautifully designed shop has been developed and crafted by artists and designers that she both knows and loves.

The ethos behind the shop's name is integral to the stock on its shelves. Whether it's a toy sailboat made from sustainable rubber wood, espresso cups thrown by a local potter or handmade soap from a small business in Leyton, every item is both sustainable and known to Karen.

With a background in interior styling and location management, it's little wonder that the shop that Karen has created is well laid out with plenty of stylish homewares to choose from. There's also a wellness corner, a children's section and an inviting terrace at the back, so you can pause amongst the greenery before heading back out on to Stoke Newington Church Street.

After Noah

121–122 Upper Street, N1 1QP
www.afternoah.com

Homeware, Furniture, Toys & Vintage

After Noah has been trading on Islington's Upper Street since 1990 but its roots go back to the late 1930s when founder Robert Keyes set up his cabinet-making and furniture restoration workshop in London's east end.

When Robert's grandson, Matthew and his wife Zoë took over the business in the 1980s, they cleverly combined vintage furniture with contemporary homewares; a style that hit a chord with interiors-savvy customers looking for industrial and reclaimed pieces.

Their fully equipped basement workshop still offers a restoration service as well as an extensive selection of mid-century furniture, antiques and vintage lighting. And in 2005, an expansion into the shop next door added space for a toyshop and the opportunity to stock contemporary furniture.

In the basement you'll find quality, restored furniture including 1960s Danish dining tables, G-Plan chairs and glass cabinets curated with vintage treasure. Back on street level, the toys, books and homewares are stylishly arranged alongside modern sofas, kitchen linens and rugs.

Marby & Elm

53 Exmouth Market, EC1R 4QL
www.marbyandelm.com

Letterpress Stationery

Marby & Elm is much more than a stationery shop; their own brand paper products are designed in-house and individually hand printed by letterpress.

Since opening the Clerkenwell shop, founder Eleanor has been joined by her brother, sister and her artist father, who creates original hand lettering for greetings cards, notecards and gift tags. Known for their love of typography and humour this family affair has attracted the likes of Liberty as well as a wide and loyal customer base.

Not your average run-of-the-mill occasion cards either; Marby & Elm's designs range from quirky to downright saucy and this, plus the handmade quality and electric colourways, means their stationery has garnered something of a cult following. Choose from the broad range of cheeky greetings and birthday cards or commission your own set of bespoke notecards.

D & A Binder

101 Holloway Road, N7 8LT
www.dandabinder.co.uk

Antiques & Bespoke Shopfittings

David Binder and his son Josh specialize in antiques and traditional shop fittings; everything from art deco cash registers to glass fronted haberdashery counters, reclaimed museum display cases, old laboratory benches, advertising signs, shop mannequins and vintage shop counters.

For the best part of forty-five years Binder's have supplied antique furniture and fittings to high end British and French clothing boutiques, as well as private clients worldwide and film and television production companies.

Their Tardis-like shop offers a vast amount of choice and a second shop, next-door-but-two, specializes in Josh's own designs. Taking inspiration from Victorian and early twentieth-century pieces, these tailor-made fittings are hand built by Josh in oak or restored mahogany at the workshop in north London.

No space for sizeable antiques? Discover some of Binder's decorative items such as vintage mirrors, lighting, glass vitrines, hat stands, Victorian brass fittings and globes – there's no end of treasure here.

Second Nature

79 Fortis Green Road, N10 3HP

Antiques & Plants

Richard Parker trained as an illustrator and went on to design books and award winning displays at Chelsea Flower Show. Second Nature is a combination of Richard's love of antiques, natural history and all things horticultural.

The shop in Muswell Hill is testament to Richard's skill as a stylist and artist and where you'll be greeted with arrangements of plants, flowers and eclectic vignettes created with illustrations of birds and butterflies, glass cases filled with old pharmacy bottles, shells and vintage curios.

It may be small scale but the shop is bristling with style. As well as antiques and plants, there's a good selection of greetings cards, candles and soft furnishings. All, of course, with a natural history theme.

SOUTH LONDON

JamJar Flowers

7A Peacock Yard, SE17 3LH
www.jamjarflowers.co.uk

Florist

JamJar flowers insist they aren't a flower shop yet passersby are constantly drawn in by the window displays of beautifully styled vintage vases and coloured glassware. Technically they operate as an events and online business but you can collect pre-ordered flowers from their Peacock Yard workshop; a Victorian cobbled mews with heaps of Dickensian character.

Inspired by the Sussex countryside, where founder Melissa Richardson grew up, JamJar uses sustainable, locally grown flowers to create romantic displays for any occasion. Treat yourself or someone special to their signature style preserve jar filled with fresh flowers and foliage.

Melissa Richardson and her team create bespoke floral designs that range from jam jars filled with seasonal flowers to large-scale events and weddings.

Tate Modern Shops

Bankside, SE1 9TG
www.tate.org.uk

Books & Gifts

Located alongside the impressive sloping entrance, the Turbine Hall shop holds Tate Modern's widest range of art-related books and products. Discover a selection of Tate Publishing's books, prints and postcards, art and design magazines and gifts inspired by contemporary art. Best for fabulously illustrated children's books and an area where young visitors are invited to sit and create.

Peruse the variety of books on culture and modern art in the Blavatnik building's shop or add to your wardrobe with a pop art printed t-shirt featuring David Hockney's *A Bigger Splash*. You'll be spoilt for choice amongst handcrafted jewellery and fashion-led gifts including sunglasses, scarves, watches and tote bags, exclusively designed around Tate's collections.

Jazz up your grocery shopping with an exclusive Tate tote bag or while away an hour or so in the Create area with younger family members (Turbine Hall shop, Level 0).

LAMP LDN

20B Maxted Road, SE15 4LF
www.lamplondonhome.com

Lifestyle & Homeware

It comes as no surprise that friends Lotte and Anna come from a background in events organization. Their lifestyle shop LAMP LDN is immaculately curated with a pitch perfect eye for detail.

When their events business was sidelined by the Covid pandemic, at the start of lockdown they took a gamble and opened a bricks and mortar shop. 'We were lucky', says Lotte, 'the double aspect windows meant that anyone walking past could see the stock, order online and collect from the doorstep without physically stepping inside.'

The shop has since gone from strength to strength and now collaborates with small-scale manufacturers and artisans to create LAMP's own range of homewares including lighting, enamelware and ceramics, as well as stocking table linens and stationery.

If you're on the look out for a living room refresh you can't go wrong with one of LAMP's candy coloured vases, cushions in bold stripes or a pair of handmade candle holders.

Brixton Cycles

296–298 Brixton Road, SW9 6AG
www.brixtoncycles.co.uk

Bicycles

Brixton Cycles is an independent co-operative run by its members, customers and community. After feeling the effects of the latest economic downturn it successfully won an appeal for crowdfunding and it's easy to see why. The sentiment and love for this long-established co-op is evident on the shop floor where staff and customers happily talk bikes, especially during the morning's busy rush hour when repairs and services are booked in or checked out.

Lincoln has been at Brixton Cycles for over thirty years and says that for him bikes and cycling, 'was always about promoting Brixton in a positive light through sport.' And you get the feeling that this attitude goes above and beyond. With the creation of an inclusive cycling club the shop also offers its customers a social side to cycling.

But back to basics; if your daily commute includes pedal power, check out their list of services from straightforward tuning to a full bike service and clean, with new parts fitted if needed. There's also a fully stocked shop with parts, accessories, locks, tyres and cycle hats, shirts and caps.

Always dreamed of your own personalized bike? Bespoke bikes, built from scratch, are the mainstay of business at Brixton Cycles and customers are invited to visit the shop to talk through their cycling needs and wants.

The Cellar Next Door

73 Camberwell Church Street, SE5 8TR
www.cellarnextdoor.com

Wine

Take three friends with a passion for food and wine, add a Michelin Bib Gourmand award and you have the makings of great bistro; so much so that it didn't stop there. Their second restaurant opened in 2019 together with The Cellar Next Door, a standalone wine shop offering rare gems and hard-to-find wines.

Founder Helen says, 'Myself, Ben and Luke choose wines we absolutely love to drink, from winemakers we adore.' They represent makers and small producers from Europe, South Africa and South America with natural and organic wines, British sparkling and orange wines – popular for their natural, macerated methods of production.

If authentic wine craftsmanship is your thing, a trip to The Cellar Next Door in Camberwell is thoroughly recommended. And while you're at it, don't forget to sample their French-influenced small plates at Little Cellars bistro next door.

Neal's Yard Dairy

8 Park Street, SE1 9AB

www.nealsyarddairy.co.uk

Cheesemonger

Neal's Yard Dairy was established in 1979 by Randolph Hodgson in an unloved corner of Covent Garden – the self titled Neal's Yard. Lacking in experience but with a passion for British cheesemaking, he embarked on farm visits around the country learning about their production methods and bringing their cheeses back to his shop.

Now working with over forty British and Irish cheesemakers and with three other London locations, including the Borough shop (opposite), Neal's Yard Dairy goes beyond just selling cheese.

They represent some of the best independent makers borne out of their commitment to the art of cheesemaking and slow production. Expect to discover regional, heritage cheeses from Cheshire, Lancashire, Wensleydale, Caerphilly, Red Leicester and many more inspired by other parts of Europe.

And don't be shy when visiting – the staff are some of the most welcoming you'll encounter. Before you know it, you'll be sampling your way through your wishlist cheeseboard.

For over forty-five years, Neal's Yard Dairy has represented the very best of British and Irish cheesemakers. In 2015 founder Randolph Hodgson won a Lifetime Achievement Award from the British Farming Awards for his commitment to British food and farming.

Borough Market

8 Southwark Street, SE1 1TL
www.boroughmarket.org.uk

Food Market

London's skyline and adjacent area may well have altered with the addition of the Shard, but Borough Market has been home to independent traders for centuries. Established in 1756 the food market came into its own in 1862 when fruit and vegetable wholesalers began trading around the newly built Victorian railway viaduct. Steeped in history and still an independent community market, the Henry Rose, Art Deco building now hosts over a hundred shops, stands and bars.

Open every day except Mondays, plan your visit around a host of culinary delights starting with coffee at Monmouth Coffee Company (2 Park St.), followed by a stroll around the market for some of the best organic produce under one roof.

Treat yourself to tapas at Brindisa (18–20 Southwark St.), book a table at Elliot's (12 Stoney St.) or linger for lunch in one of the many other restaurants and bars.

For an early evening aperitif soak up the atmosphere at Bedales of Borough or Borough Wines (open until 5pm) and before you leave, pick up speciality breads and cakes at The Flour Station and wedges of cheese from Neal's Yard Dairy.

The stand at Hickson & Daughter laden with fresh fruit and vegetables.

Shops by Category

Directory

After Noah
121–122 Upper Street,
N1 1QP
www.afternoah.com
see page 110

Bob & Blossom
140 Columbia Road, E2 7RG
www.bobandblossom.co.uk
see page 28

Brixton Cycles
296–298 Brixton Road,
SW9 6AG
www.brixtoncycles.co.uk
see page 128

Broadway Market
London, E8
www.broadwaymarket.co.uk
see page 22

Canford & Co.
307 Lillie Road, SW6 7LL
www.canfordframes.co.uk
see page 56

Cecil Court
WC2, www.cecilcourt.co.uk
see page 83

Ceramica Blue
10 Blenheim Crescent,
W11 1NN
www.ceramicablue.co.uk
see page 52

Colours of Arley
61 Hackney Road, E2 7NX
www.coloursofarley.com
see page 38

Columbia Road
Columbia Road, E2
www.columbiaroad.info
see page 27

Columbia Road Flower Market
Columbia Road, E2 7RG
www.columbiaroadmarket.co.uk
see page 25

Conservatory Archives
3–7 Lower Clapton Road,
E5 0NS
www.conservatoryarchives.co.uk
see page 30

D & A Binder
101 Holloway Road, N7 8LT
www.dandabinder.co.uk
see page 114

David Mellor
190 Pavilion Road, SW3 2BF
www.davidmellordesign.com
see page 48

David Penton & Son
64 Marylebone Lane,
W1U 2PE
www.pentonshardware.co.uk
see page 74

Giddy Grocer
80 Bermondsey Street,
SE1 3UD
www.giddygrocer.co.uk
see page 2

JamJar Flowers
7A Peacock Yard, SE17 3LH
www.jamjarflowers.co.uk
see page 120

Jessica de Lotz
49 Fortess Rd, NW5 1AD
www.jessicadelotz.co.uk
see page 105

John Sandoe Books
10–12 Blacklands Terrace,
SW3 2SR
www.johnsandoe.com
see page 60

Know & Love
176 Stoke Newington
Church Street, N16 0JL
www.knowandlove.co.uk
see page 108

L Cornelissen & Son
105 Great Russell Street,
WC1B 3RW
www.cornelissen.com
see page 78

LF Markey
50 Dalston Lane, E8 3AH
www.lfmarkey.com
see page 12

La Fromagerie
52 Lamb's Conduit Street,
WC1N 3LL
www.lafromagerie.co.uk
see page 88

Lamp LDN
20B Maxted Road, SE15 4LF
www.lamplondonhome.com
see page 126

London Review Bookshop
14 Bury Place, WC1A 2JL
www.londonreviewbookshop.co.uk
see page 86

Loop
15 Camden Passage, N1 8EA
www.loopknitting.com
see page 98

Lutyens & Rubinstein
21 Kensington Park Road,
W11 2EU
www.landrbookshop.co.uk
see page 54

M Charpentier Antiques
284 Lillie Road, SW6 7PX
www.mcharpentier.com
see page 62

Marby & Elm
53 Exmouth Market,
EC1R 4QL
www.marbyandelm.com
see page 112

Milagros
61 Columbia Road, E2 7RG
www.milagros.co.uk
see page 16

Mr Jones Watches
53a Neal Street, WC2H 9PJ
www.mrjoneswatches.com
see page 84

My Little Garden
158 Liverpool Rd,
Old Concertina Works,
N1 1LA
@mylittlegardenlondon
See page 96

N1 Garden Centre
25A Englefield Road, N1 4EU
www.n1gardencentre.co.uk
see page 102

Neal's Yard Dairy
8 Park Street, SE1 9AB
www.nealsyarddairy.co.uk
see page 134

O Pioneers
76 Marylebone Lane,
W1U 2PR
www.opioneers.co.uk
see page 72

Panter & Hall
22–24 Cecil Court,
WC2N 4HE and
21–22 Pall Mall, SW1Y 5LP
www.panterandhall.com
see page 80

Papers & Paints
4 Park Walk, SW10 0AD
www.papersandpaints.co.uk
see page 50

Papersmiths
170 Pavilion Road,
SW1X 0AW
www.papersmiths.co.uk
see page 44

Paul Rothe & Son
35 Marylebone Lane,
W1U 2NN,
@paulrotheandson
see page 66

Postcard Teas
9 Dering Street, W1S 1AG
www.postcardteas.com
see page 68

Regent Sounds
4 Denmark Street, WC2H 8LP
www.regentsounds.com
see page 64

Retrouvé
61 Wilton Way, E8 1BG
www.retrouvevintage.co.uk
see page 10

Second Nature
79 Fortis Green Road, N10 3HP
see page 116

Sir John Soane's Museum
13 Lincoln's Inn Fields,
WC2A 3BP
www.soane.org
see page 77

Studio Wylder
67 Columbia Road, E2 7RG
www.studiowylder.com
see page 20

Summerill & Bishop
100 Portland Road, W11 4LQ
and 58 Elizabeth Street,
SW1W 9PB
www.summerillandbishop.com
see page 46

Tate Modern Shops
Bankside, SE1 9TG
www. tate.org.uk
see page 124

The Cellar Next Door
73 Camberwell Church
Street, SE5 8TR
www.cellarnextdoor.com
see page 132

The Deli Downstairs
211 Victoria Park Road, E9 7JN
www.thedelidownstairs.co.uk
see page 34

The Mercantile
17a Lamb Street, E1 6EA
www.themercantilelondon.com
see page 36

Violet Cakes
47 Wilton Way, E8 3ED
www.violetcakes.com
see page 14

Wild at Heart
Liberty, Great Marlborough
Street, W1B 5AH
www.wildatheart.com
see page 92

Yeast
Unit 1 Canal Place,
1–3 Sheep Lane, E8 4QS
www.yeastbakery.com
see page 18

Acknowledgements

I would like to thank all at Pimpernel Press and Gemini for making this book happen especially to Jo, Gail and Adrian for the opportunity. To my editor Anna, always a pleasure to work with you and very special thanks to Nicki for the design.

Huge thanks goes to each and every shopkeeper featured in the book for your time and generosity and for giving me behind the scenes access to your shops and stories. It's been a joy to discover – and rediscover – both new and long established independent businesses and to reacquaint myself with my home city.

I've met so many inspiring people whilst working on the project and it wouldn't have been possible without their input and kindness.

Thank you,
Michelle

Picture credits

Published in 2025
by Gemini Books Ltd
Part of Gemini Books Group

Based in Woodbridge and London

Marine House, Tide Mill Way,
Woodbridge, SUFFOLK IP12 1AP
United Kingdom

www.geminibooks.com

ISBN 9781914902215

A CIP catalogue record for this book is available from the British Library.

Designed by Nicki Davis
Typeset in Garamond and Verdigris

Every reasonable effort has been made to trace copyright-holders of material reproduced in this book,
but if any have been inadvertently overlooked the publishers would be glad to hear from them.

Printed in China
10 9 8 7 6 5 4 3 2 1